HOW WE
USED TO LIVE
IN AUSTRALIA

FOOD AND COOKING

Rachel Dixon

First published 2018 by
Redback Publishing
PO Box 357 Frenchs Forest NSW 2086
Australia

www.redbackpublishing.com.au
orders@redbackpublishing.com.au

978-1-925630-32-9

Author: Rachel Dixon
Editor: Marianne Lindsell
Designer: Redback Publishing

Original illustrations © Redback Publishing 2018
Originated by Redback Publishing

Printed and bound in China by Leo Paper

FSC
www.fsc.org
MIX
Paper from responsible sources
FSC® C020056

Acknowledgements
Abbreviations: l—left, r—right, b—bottom, t—top, c—centre, m—middle
We would like to thank the following for permission to reproduce photographs: (Images © shutterstock) p5mr By Bjørn Christian Tørrissen [CC BY-SA 3.0 (https://creativecommons.org/licenses/by-sa/3.0) or GFDL (http://www.gnu.org/copyleft/fdl.html)], via Wikimedia Commons, P7B The collections of the State Library of New South Wales, p10 Museums Victoria, p11t State Library of New South Wales, p11bl Sharon Wills, p13ml State Library of Victoria, p13mr Argus Newspaper Collection of Photographs, State Library of Victoria, p14b By State Library of New South Wales collection [No restrictions], via Wikimedia Commons, p15br Museums Victoria Collections, p16 State Library of Victoria, p24t Isewell [CC BY-SA 2.5 (https://creativecommons.org/licenses/by-sa/2.5)], via Wikimedia Commons, p28bl Museums Victoria Collections

A catalogue record for this book is available from the National Library of Australia

CONTENTS

TRADITIONAL AUSTRALIAN ABORIGINAL FOODS

FROM 60,000 YEARS AGO TO THE PRESENT

WHAT FOODS DID THE FIRST AUSTRALIAN ABORIGINAL PEOPLE EAT?

Australian Aboriginal people arrived in Australia about 60,000 years ago. They probably collected fruit, seeds and vegetables, hunted animals and fished in oceans, lakes and rivers. When they arrived, Australia's megafauna were still alive. These animals included giant wombats, birds and a large meat-eating kangaroo. People hunted these megafauna for food. Palaeontologists who study the ancient megafauna are not sure if they became extinct because of being hunted or due to climate change thousands of years ago.

Australian Aboriginal people who live a traditional lifestyle today still gather plants, seeds and vegetable foods and hunt or fish for meat.

WHERE DID FOOD COME FROM?

Animals hunted for their meat were caught using spears, boomerangs and clubs. Aboriginal people did not keep herds of animals, but hunted wild creatures when they needed them for food. Stone traps built in rivers made fishing easier.

Aboriginal people knew that taking too much food from the one area could result in the death of the plants they needed and the loss of the animals they hunted. To ensure that food would always be available, they moved away from areas over time, hunting and gathering food elsewhere to avoid overusing any resource.

TRADITIONAL BUSH FOODS FROM THE DESERT	
PLANTS	• Quandongs • Yams • Bush tomatoes, plums, apples, raisins and limes • Lemon myrtle • Wattle and grass seeds which can be ground and baked
INSECTS	• Grubs and caterpillars • Honey ants • Bee honey
MEAT	• Small mammals

HOW WAS FOOD PREPARED AND KEPT?

Over thousands of years, Aboriginal people discovered what foods were safe to eat, and developed cooking methods that made some poisonous plants edible. Meat, yams and root vegetables were cooked in campfires or in earth ovens.

People fishing in their canoes sometimes kept a small fire going that could be used to cook fish immediately without having to return to land to eat.

Grinding stones and slabs were used to grind seeds into flour, which was then baked into a flat bread. Archaeologists have found grinding stones in Australia that are 30,000 years old. Seeds used to make bread came from grasses, spinifex and wattle plants. The time consuming task of gathering and grinding seeds would have involved mostly women and children.

Weaving and knotting to make carry bags was the role of women. They used their bags to carry food, tools and utensils, including their important grinding stones.

Aboriginal and Torres Strait Islander people used agriculture, grew plants and developed farming techniques that included irrigation and harvesting seeds.

SWEET TREATS

Ripe fruits, honey ants and honeycomb from bees were sweet treats that were only available in certain seasons, or when a beehive could be found.

WHAT DID THEY DRINK?

In the arid areas of Australia, Aboriginal people developed ways of communicating to others the location of water springs and wells. The traditional art style, as well as the songs kept by the Elders helped to make sure everyone in the group knew where to find water in the desert. Some plant roots and stems store water, and Aboriginal people discovered which of these were good to drink and which ones were poisonous.

WASTE DISPOSAL

Ancient shell middens and bone piles are found throughout Australia. The shells and bones in middens are the leftover waste from meals enjoyed by Aboriginal people thousands of years ago. The rest of their food scraps were biodegradable.

NSW, 1817.

CONVICTS OF THE FIRST FLEET

WHAT FOODS DID THE EARLY CONVICTS EAT?

When the first convicts and their guards arrived in Australia in 1788, they did not realise that the bush was full of delicious, edible foods. At first they lived off the foods that had been brought with them in their ships. These foods included flour, dried peas and salted meat.

There was no fresh fruit left. Some convicts gathered green leaves that looked like the spinach they were used to eating back in England. They also killed wallabies and other animals for meat and fished in Sydney harbour.

Despite the abundance of food sources around them, the convicts and early settlers all nearly starved. It took them 25 years to overcome the constant shortage of food.

WHERE DID FOOD COME FROM?

The small amount of food that was left over in 1788 from the sea voyage was carefully stored. Convicts who stole any of it were executed. Small gardens were planted with seeds brought from Britain. The food was rationed, and everyone had to wait two years before another ship arrived, bringing them more food. However, by the late 1790s, the convicts and settlers were growing crops of wheat and keeping sheep and cattle. In 1813, the settlers sent a message to Britain saying that there was no need to send them any more salted meat, as they were finally producing enough fresh meat for themselves in the colony.

HOW WAS FOOD PREPARED AND KEPT?

The preserved food that came on ships from England was made into a salty stew or soup. Each convict was given his or her own ration and had to cook it themselves over a campfire. There was no way to keep meat fresh if they killed an animal or caught a fish, so it had to be eaten right away.

For many years, grain was kept in government storehouses. Theft of food from houses or from other people's garden plots was a serious crime.

WHAT DID THEY DRINK?

Because of the poor quality of drinking water in London, the early convicts were used to drinking alcohol instead. Even children drank alcohol mixed with water. In the colony they continued this habit of not trusting fresh water. Rum was traded amongst people instead of money, and it was used to pay wages and to buy things.

WASTE DISPOSAL

The people from the First Fleet used the water of the Tank Stream as their dumping ground for rubbish and sewage. The stream soon became polluted and unusable as a source of water for drinking or washing.

Old Tank Stream Sydney, 1852.

COLONIAL SETTLERS IN THE MID 1800s

WHAT FOODS DID PEOPLE EAT?

The first Australian cookbook appeared in 1864. Its food was very British in style, although kangaroo and wombat were included in the ingredients. There were no take away shops as we know today, but people could buy pies, cakes, bread and sweets to take home. Rabbits had been released into the bush and they were hunted and sold for their meat. Rabbit stew and rabbit pies were popular and cheap to make.

Food was generally natural and healthy, but there were some ingredients that would not be allowed today. Dangerous chemicals were added to colour and to preserve some foods. These chemicals contained cyanides and compounds of lead, copper and mercury, all lethal in large doses. Some farmers added chalk to their milk.

WHERE DID FOOD COME FROM?

By the mid 1800s, Australia was a major producer of food. Shops sold local produce and imported goods from around the world. Most people kept a vegetable garden, but there were many shops selling food. Preserved foods from Britain were expensive and considered delicacies. These included jams and dried fruits. Spices still had to be imported, mostly from India and Asia.

FAST FACT

Curries have been a part of the Australian diet since the 1800s. Australia's close trading connection with India during colonial times led to some Indian foods becoming popular amongst the local settlers.

HOW WAS FOOD PREPARED AND KEPT?

Canned food was becoming acceptable. Refrigeration had been invented and this was used by businesses, although ordinary people did not have refrigerators. People with large houses had cellars where food was stored to keep it cool. The only way to make jellies set in the summer was to place them in the cellar where the air was cool. People who lived in small houses and huts had no way of way of keeping food cool in the summer, or of storing perishable food like meat or bread.

Insect pests, rats and mice were in most homes. To keep mice out of food, meat and bread were kept in a box that was hung from the ceiling. Some people used specially constructed 'food safes' with walls made of wire mesh.

The kitchen in small houses was often built separately from the main house, because fires caused by cooking were so common. The chimney over the fireplace where people cooked became very hot and had to be separated from the wooden walls of the house. In large houses, the kitchen was a big room, often with more than one oven, fed by either wood or coal.

WHAT DID THEY DRINK?

Tea was costly and wealthy people kept it in locked boxes to stop the servants taking it. Today, these tea boxes are valuable antiques. Factories making soft drinks produced ginger beer, cordial and fizzy drinks. The bottles kept their fizz by using a glass marble, which helped seal the top from the inside.

WASTE DISPOSAL

Glass, tin cans and pottery from ginger beer bottles are often found in rubbish dumps from the 1800s. Many of these items are now collectable antiques. One of the earliest council rubbish collection services operated in Melbourne in the 1860s. In other areas, people buried their rubbish on their properties, or found some vacant land where they either dumped or buried it. Burning of household rubbish was common.

Colonial Australians ate many foods that we do not see on our plates today

• black swans • wombats • dugongs • echidnas • possums • parrots

Today we eat foods that colonial Australians would have thought were very unusual

• Olive Oil For Cooking • Tomato Sauce In Plastic Bottles • Spaghetti Bolognaise • Pad Thai • Pizza • Fried Ice Cream • Yum Cha • Sliced Bread • Sushi • Fast Food Hamburgers • Doner Kebabs • Hot Dogs • Falafel • Packets Of Potato Crisps • Mexican Tacos • Packaged Frozen Dinners

FOOD AND COOKING IN THE EARLY 1900s

WHAT FOODS DID PEOPLE EAT?

Australia developed its standard meal of meat and vegetables, with puddings, cakes and biscuits for dessert and snacks. Foods such as pasta and fried rice were unknown in most homes.

WHERE DID FOOD COME FROM?

Shoppers buying groceries waited to be served by a shop assistant. They could not go to the shelves and pick items for themselves. Biscuits, flour and rice were not packaged. The grocer would measure out the amount the customer asked for and put it in a paper bag or in the customer's own container. Home delivery was offered by the 'grocer's boy' on his bicycle, or the grocer used a horse and cart. In the arid parts of Australia, Afghan cameleers provided a home delivery service to isolated homes.

Butcher shops used to hang their meat outside the shop so that people passing by could see what they had available.

Milk was sold from a large can and people would bring their own containers to be filled. Children would often have the job of going to the dairy or the bakery to buy the milk or bread for the family.

Australia had to produce most of its own fresh food, because of the long travel times from any other country. Nearly all rice consumed was still imported.

Victoria, 1900s.

HOW WAS FOOD PREPARED AND KEPT?

In families, women and girls did most of the cooking and shopping. This was considered a very important role, and courses in home cooking and domestic management were offered to train girls for their future role as housewives.

SA, grocery store built in 1854.

SWEET TREATS

With advances in refrigeration, ice-creams became cheaper and more widely available. Ice-creams were sold from the back of a cart pulled by a horse.

WHEAT

In the late 1800s, the wheat harvest in Australia had suffered due to the fungal disease called rust. In 1900, William Farrer developed a new type of wheat that was resistant to this disease. His discovery resulted in a large increase in the size of Australia's wheat crop, making the country one of the world's leading producers of wheat.

Australian
ANZAC biscuits

ANZACS AND THE FIRST WORLD WAR

The Anzac soldiers fighting in Turkey had a very restricted diet. Their main food was tinned meat called bully beef, hard biscuits, tea and sugar. There was little fresh fruit and few vegetables. This resulted in many men developing diseases caused by a lack of vitamin C. There was no fresh water supply for the troops fighting at Gallipoli. Their water was carried in containers from their ships, and the enemy shot at the soldiers as they brought the food and water supplies to the troops. The saltiness of their food, combined with rationed drinking water, would have caused them to be constantly thirsty.

ANZAC BISCUITS

The Australian soldiers who fought during the First World War in Europe and Turkey probably did not eat Anzac biscuits. The recipe for this iconic biscuit was developed back in Australia and the biscuits were sold to raise funds for the war effort.

AUSTRALIAN COMFORTS FUND

This organisation of volunteers, most of them women, raised funds and packed parcels of food and other items for the fighting soldiers. The parcel contents included plum pudding, condensed milk, chocolate and any foods that would not spoil in the heat and that would survive the long sea voyage from Australia.

SENDING FOOD TO BRITAIN

Australia donated food to Britain to feed both the British people and the Belgian refugees who had escaped the war in their own country. Local councils in Britain distributed tinned mutton from Australia to needy families. Some Australian farmers planted extra wheat to supply Britain's need during the war.

GREAT DEPRESSION 1930s

WHAT FOODS DID PEOPLE EAT?

Many Australians were unemployed during the Great Depression of the 1930s, and could not afford to buy much food. Instead of buying butter, poor people used meat fat, called dripping, spread on bread with jam. Margarine was first sold in Australia in the 1930s as a cheaper alternative to butter. Unemployed men would try to earn some money by catching wild rabbits and selling them. Anyone with a fruit tree might travel from house to house trying to sell their fruit. Children were often hungry and the whole family would have to wait for the father to find some sort of work so they could buy food. Women frequently sold or pawned their wedding rings to get money to feed their families.

Anything that grew naturally and was edible was gathered and eaten: wild mushrooms, thistles to make soup, dandelions to make herbal tea. People sometimes became very ill from eating things that were not edible, like poisonous mushrooms. A chicken was a prized possession because it laid eggs, but it also had to be protected from being stolen and eaten by a hungry person.

The poorest families could not afford rent and moved to live in 'shanty towns', made up of tents or simple huts. They cooked over open fires and usually had nowhere to grow their own food. Hungry people stole food from gardens, so maintaining a vegetable patch for the family during this time was a difficult task.

During the Great Depression. Governments offered poor people and their families 'food relief' tickets, which they took to distribution centres to get free food. The term 'dole' was used to describe these government handouts. This word is still used to refer to social security benefits today.

Amongst some people who were not suffering hunger during the Depression, the 'Hobo Party' was a popular theme, where party guests dressed up like poor people.

Schoolchildren lining up for free soup and a slice of bread. Sydney, 1934.

Men in a dole queue. Sydney, 1931.

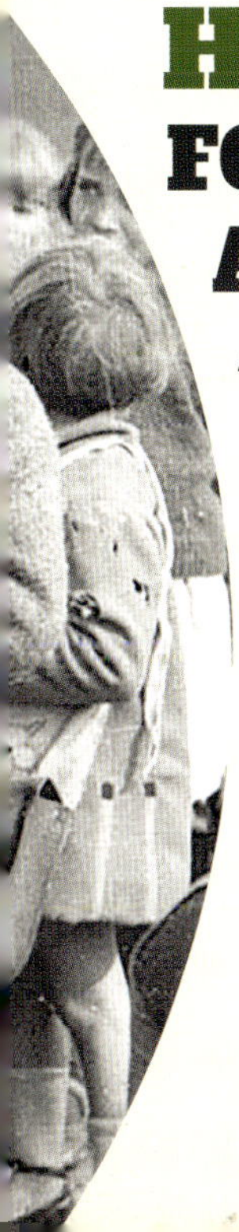

HOW WAS FOOD PREPARED AND KEPT?

At the beginning of the 1900s there was gas and electricity for kitchen gadgets, but during the Great Depression many poor people had to go back to cooking over a wood fire. People who could not pay power bills had to gather firewood instead.

SWEET TREATS

Sweets and lollies were an expensive luxury for people who could not afford to buy food. Some mothers would make sweets for their children by boiling a small amount of sugar and pouring it into jar lid moulds to make toffees.

SECOND WORLD WAR FOOD RATIONING

Food shortages caused by the Second World War meant that food had to be rationed from 1943 right up until after the war in 1950. People received ration booklets, which they had to show to shopkeepers before they could buy rationed foods.

Woman studying her new ration book
Melbourne, 1943.

FOODS RATIONED

Butter, Tea, Sugar, Meat, Eggs, Milk

Many other foods were also difficult to get because agricultural production decreased when so many men were away fighting in the war. The shortage of tea led to the production of other drinks as a substitute. Coffee became more popular, as well as coffee substitutes, such as chicory or roasted wheat.

Some of the rationing was to make sure supplies of foods, such as butter, could be sent to Britain, where food was scarce during the war. The heavy bombing suffered by the Londoners made the government of Australia decide that it had to help them by sending food, even though Australians themselves were experiencing rationing.

Housewives were encouraged to make meals out of leftovers and not to waste anything. One wartime recipe involved mincing up leftover sandwiches and baking them in an oven to make the main course for dinner.

Although inner city dwellers suffered because of rationing, country people ate better meals as they had more room to keep chickens and grow vegetables.

Rationing encouraged the rise of a 'black market' that sold food and other goods that had been stolen or obtained illegally.

FOOD AND COOKING IN THE 1950s

After the Second World War, the pre-war ways of cooking were considered old fashioned and people wanted modern kitchens and appliances. The United States rather than Britain became the style leader, and Australian families wanted households and meals that were more like the ones they saw in American television shows.

SOME OF THE FEATURES OF FOOD AND COOKING IN THE 1950s:

- Frozen vegetables could be used since most houses now had refrigerators.
- Advertising promoted the American style of kitchen with lots of electric gadgets and everything stored neatly and hidden from view in cupboards.
- Self-service supermarkets allowed customers to touch the goods before buying them. There was often just one checkout.
- Chinese restaurants, Greek milk bars and European coffee shops brought a different style of eating out. People still enjoyed visiting teashops, cafes selling plain foods, and big cafeterias provided in large department stores.
- Milk and bread continued to be delivered to suburban homes in a horse and cart.
- Nearly all shops were closed on the weekends and after 5 o'clock on weekdays, so shopping had to be done at other times.
- Most women worked in the home rather than in jobs outside, which allowed them to do their grocery shopping during the day.

EATING AT SCHOOL

- School lunches consisted of white bread sandwiches, fruit, cakes, lollies, cordial, meat pies or sausage rolls.
- Children from the migrant families who came to Australia after the end of the Second World War in Europe brought different foods that other children had never seen before. These foods included salami, olives, parmesan cheese, black rye bread drizzled with flavoured olive oil instead of spread with butter or margarine, chocolate crepes as treats, and bottled mineral water.
- The Government promoted the Oslo Lunch as the best lunch for school children. It included cheese and salad on wholemeal bread and a daily drink of milk.
- Governments provided free milk for school children. Some children enjoyed drinking it but others hated being forced to drink warm milk that had been sitting in bottles outside until it was time for recess. Straws with flavouring inside them became popular as a way of improving the taste of the milk as it was sucked though the straw.

MODERN FOODS

The biggest difference in modern food and cooking is that people know how to cook foods from a variety of different cultures. A wok is no longer a rarity in an Australian kitchen, and most people know how to make a stir-fry. Falafel, satays, sushi and many more wonderful foods are now enjoyed everywhere in Australia. In fact, consumers expect to be able to buy a variety of international foods wherever they live.

Pizzas first became popular in the 1960s and 1970s. Supermarkets promoted fast foods to take home to eat as family meals. The BBQ chicken makes a popular quick meal, as many parents do not have the time to spend roasting a chicken at home.

Cooking is now a family role and not just a household job for women. Kitchens in modern houses are no longer separated from the living area by a closed door, encouraging everyone in the family to take a part in food preparation.

Food preparation has become an activity for celebrities. Even children know the names of famous top chefs, and cooking on television shows provides a subject for discussion at school and at work.

EATING AT SCHOOL

Despite all the research that scientists have done on the healthiest foods to eat, children at many schools are still drinking cans of sugary drink at lunch, and eating salty chips and other foods that should only be eaten rarely if at all. School canteens are expected to provide healthy foods and restrict the sugary and salty snacks that used to be commonly available.

Children now enjoy bringing lunches to school that have a variety of ingredients used by different cultures and nationalities. Many schools now grow their own foods in kitchen gardens and the children learn to cook seasonal foods.

WASTE DISPOSAL

Burning of rubbish has been banned in most city areas and the backyard incinerator is no longer used. Recycling is a necessity and local governments spend large amounts of ratepayers' funds on rubbish removal and recycling. Gigantic rubbish dumps still use burial in pits as the major way of disposing of household garbage.

Despite the widespread desire by most people to take care of the environment, the huge amounts of plastic used in the food industry make its safe disposal difficult.

THE AUSSIE BBQ

The Australian outdoor BBQ is one of the most popular ways to prepare a meal. Although Australians like to claim the BBQ as their own invention, it is more likely that it originated in America.

THE FUTURE OF FOOD

WHERE WILL FOOD COME FROM?

WHERE WILL FOOD COME FROM?

- Genetically modified plants and animals may be needed to produce the huge amounts of food required to feed the increasing world population.
- More genetically modified foods will be owned by businesses that will not allow anyone else to produce them.
- Insects and algae could be farmed for human food.
- Bees are dying around the world. We all depend on bees to pollinate the plant foods we eat and that also feed livestock. If bee numbers decrease, an alternate method of pollination will be needed.
- Improved preservation methods will allow exports from parts of the world that may eventually become specialist food producers for the whole planet.
- Increasing world population will mean that more farming land is used for housing instead. People may return to the old idea of everyone growing their own food in whatever space they have, either in a garden or in pots on a balcony.

HOW WILL FOOD BE PREPARED AND KEPT?

- 3D printing of fast foods, sweets and treats could become a reality.
- There may be increased use of prepared foods that are delivered to homes and require only heating.
- Scientists may invent advanced methods of storing food so that it can be grown during good seasons and still be available to consumers during periods of drought or flood, when agricultural produce is reduced.

WHAT WILL PEOPLE DRINK?

Clean water is a precious resource. In the arid parts of Australia, the water supply is already scarce, and people and livestock rely on drawing underground water from artesian basins. Underground water can be contaminated by careless human activity that causes waste and pollution to enter the artesian storage areas. Australia's drinking water will have to be carefully managed as the population increases.

ORGANIC FOODS

A reliance on prepared and chemically altered foods may result in an organic revolution. People who can afford to buy foods grown and prepared completely naturally may turn away from mass produced foods created with chemicals or genetically modified forms of plants and animals.

WASTE DISPOSAL

Plastic and polystyrene food packaging will overwhelm rubbish dumps and pollute land and waterways unless their production and use is controlled in the future. People will need to consider whether the packaging around the food they buy is unnecessary or too damaging to the environment.

WHAT DO YOU THINK?

- **Will drones or driverless vehicles home deliver food?**
- **Could meat come from cloned animal cells rather than from a slaughtered animal?**

TIMELINE OF CREATING HEAT FOR COOKING

PRE-HISTORIC ERAS

Fire was produced by friction when rubbing wooden sticks together. Flint stones were used to produce sparks when struck.

FIRST SETTLERS 1788

Flint stones were still being used to produce sparks when struck.

1799

Coal was found in Newcastle and shipped to the new settlement at Sydney Cove where it was burnt for cooking and for heating.

MID 1800s

First matches sold.

1873

First gas stove imported into Australia.

1906

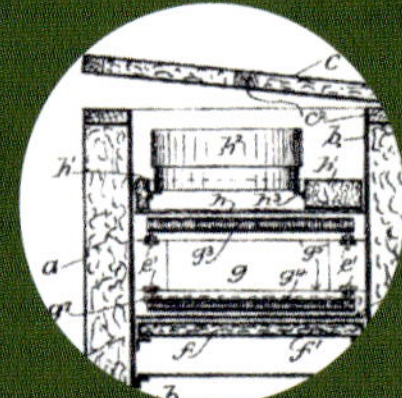

The Kalgoorlie Stove was the first electric stove designed and made in Australia. Its inventor was David Curle Smith.

1970s

The first microwave ovens were sold but many people would not use them because they thought the microwaves were too dangerous.

TIMELINE OF FIRSTS IN AUSTRALIAN KITCHENS

FIRST PLASTIC KITCHEN UTENSILS – 1930s

FIRST ICE BOXES USED TO STORE FOOD – 1839: ice imported in ships from North America

FIRST REFRIGERATORS – 1920s: gas as a power source

FIRST ELECTRIC FOOD MIXERS – early 1900s

FIRST POPULAR DISHWASHING MACHINES – mid 1950s

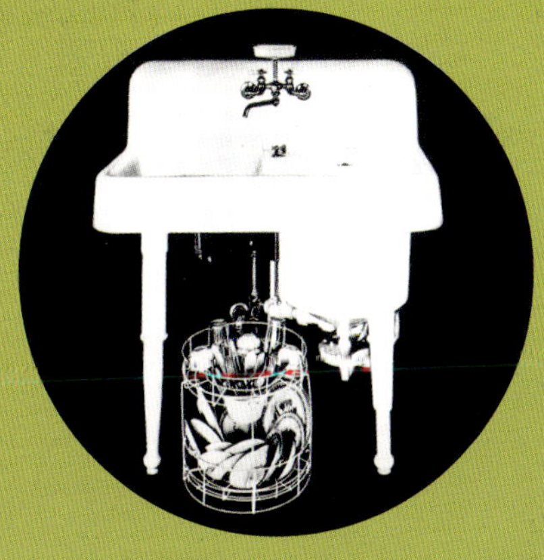

TIMELINE OF DRINKING WATER SOURCES

PRE-HISTORIC ERAS	Natural water sources - rivers, lakes, springs, rain
FIRST SETTLERS 1788	The Tank Stream in Sydney
1820s	Water delivered around Sydney in carts
1800s	Natural water sources - rivers, lakes, springs, rain, wells with pumps
1844	First 70 houses in Sydney had pipes connected to water supply
FROM MID 1800s	Dams on rivers
1980s	Bottled water from shops gained popularity
2006	Large-scale seawater desalination
TODAY	In rural areas, many people rely on water from wells and rainwater. In times of drought, they still need to have water delivered in water tank trucks

HISTORY OF TOAST

TRADITIONAL AUSTRALIAN ABORIGINAL COOKING
Flat breads made from ground seeds can be cooked over a camp fire and made crispy in the fire

CONVICTS FROM 1788
Bread toasted on a stick over a camp fire

Many people eat toast every day. The simple act of toasting and buttering a piece of bread has a long history. People did not always make it the way we do today.

SETTLERS FROM THE LATE 1700s ONWARDS
Bread placed in a metal holder called a hearth grill, which was placed over the flames of the stove

EARLY 1900s
First electric toasters used

MID 1900s
Electric toasters are expensive and repaired if they break down

TODAY
Cheap electric toasters are thrown away if they break down and replaced with a new one

BUTTER OR MARGARINE ON TOAST?

In 1893, the Victorian government passed the Margarine Act, which made it illegal to add a yellow colour into margarine so that it looked like butter. The Act was meant to protect buyers from having margarine sold to them when they thought they were buying butter. It also protected the butter industry from having to compete with margarine makers.

The labelling on margarine packaging had to be a set size to stop producers from printing the contents in very small type. If any margarine was found that did not meet these requirements, the government could take it all and destroy it.

EATING OUT AND FAST FOOD

Eating at restaurants and cafes is nothing new. Australians have been eating out since the early days of the first settlement.

EARLY SETTLERS

The British convicts and early settlers who had come from London were used to eating out. Poor people lived in single rooms with little space for cooking. They were accustomed to buying food from street sellers. Those with some money to spare frequented teashops, while wealthy people enjoyed restaurants run by the celebrity chefs of the 1800s.

In Australia, ex-convict women set up food shops supplying dishes that were mainly composed of meat, vegetables and simple puddings. Chinese men who came to Australia, attracted by the gold rush, set up the first Chinese cafes. The food they served was mostly British in style.

Hotels served meals as well as alcohol. With no fast food outlets, travellers relied on these hotels to feed them as they journeyed from town to town. They also relied on them to provide feed for their horses.

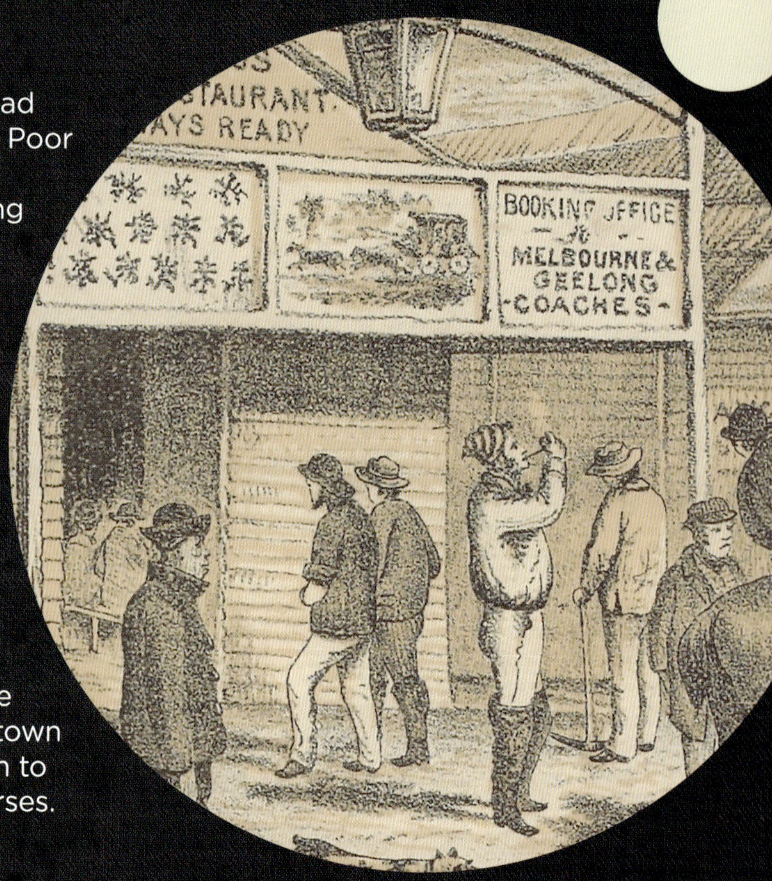

LATE 1800s

Tea and coffee shops developed into glamorous places, where customers went to be seen. In Sydney, the Chinese businessman, Quong Tart, opened teashops and fashionable English-style restaurants.

Children in restaurants were expected to sit still and behave perfectly. Noisiness or tantrums were not allowed, and children had to quietly eat what was chosen for them by the adults.

AFTER THE SECOND WORLD WAR

Australians began to experience the foods and cooking styles of people from countries other than Britain. The large numbers of migrants who came to Australia after the Second World War introduced the locals to tastes and ingredients they had never known before. Many of these new foods are now a standard part of the Australian daily diet. The new migrants often opened restaurants, cafes, milk bars and takeaway food shops, allowing others to experience their recipes and enjoy different foods.

The sharing of new food and cooking ideas is one of the ways migrants and other Australians have all developed into such a culturally harmonious nation.

FAST FOOD TODAY

Fast food restaurants today are designed to attract whole families and to allow children to be a bit noisy and active. They cater for children's tastes in foods, and they offer kids' parties and playgrounds.

CELEBRITY CHEFS

Australians follow celebrity chefs and their cooking styles on social media and television. Cooking competitions on television, where ordinary people try to cook like professionals, are very popular with children. This has resulted in children today knowing more about the secrets of cooking than probably at any other time in Australia's history. Many teenagers delight in the treat of being taken to a celebrity chef's restaurant for a special occasion, and they are able to review the meal's taste and quality in a way that young people have never done before.

FEEDING OUR PETS

Pet food now comes in plastic bags and cans, but this wasn't always the way we fed our animal friends.

Pet dogs and cats used to eat mostly food scraps. Dogs might get a bone from the butcher and sometimes people would buy meat off-cuts for them. Meat has become so expensive, that even these little pieces of meat are now sold for humans to eat. Working dogs on farms have always been valuable for their skills with livestock. Because of this, farmers have fed them well.

Cats used to be expected to keep mice under control, and other food was given to them to supplement their diet, not to replace it. In the early colony, cats and kittens arrived on ships and were sold for very high prices, both as pets and for their role as pest exterminators.

Pet birds were very popular right from the days of the first settlement. Prepared seed mixes have been available for sale from at least the 1890s.

Prepared pet foods are now promoted as the best source of the vitamins and minerals that a domestic animal requires. Labelling has developed so that the buyer now knows what is in the can or bag of food they are buying. Global companies produce the majority of pet food, and making food for domestic animals is an important industry in Australia.

FAST FACT

Whale meat used to be allowed as pet food

GLOSSARY

Archaeologist .... Person who studies remains left by human activity

Biodegradable .... Decomposing into natural substances

Cloning .... Producing life by copying a cell from a living thing

Genetically modified food ... Food which has had it's genes altered by scientists

Megafauna .... Large, prehistoric animals

Mutton .... Meat from sheep

Paleontologist .... Person who studies fossils

Ratepayer .... Person who owns a property and pays money to a local council for services

Shell midden .... Ancient rubbish pile of shells

To pawn .... To give something to a money-lender in return for money

INDEX